About

Sexual OCD is a type of OCD that is never talked about, however it is extremely common. The reason why it is not commonly discussed is because people see something bad or embarrassing in talking about this type of OCD. I am here to tell you that Sexual OCD is not that different from any other type of OCD. There is nothing shameful about it. The fact that you currently have this type of OCD does not change who you are and does not make you a bad person. It is simply a type of OCD. It is possible to overcome it.

In this book we will discuss in detail how to get over OCD. We will also go over the details of overcoming Sexual OCD in particular. These details are important because you need to understand exactly where these thoughts and fears come from so you stop being in fear of them. I truly believe that in order to overcome OCD you need to become an expert in this disorder. You need to understand why you are having these thoughts, feelings and fears.

After reading this book you will have all the tools you need to overcome OCD. Please make sure to complete the second portion of the book, which is the practical application of everything you learned.

My OCD Story

I have been suffering with OCD for many years before I created a method of how to get over it. I am not a doctor. I am not a professional writer. I hope you keep this second part in mind as you read this book. This is not a book to read and put away. I have helped many people get over OCD and I can tell you that this method works as long as you apply it.

When I was suffering with OCD I never thought I would get over it. I could not even imagine that not only I would get over it, but I would be helping others with it as well. You can get over this. You can recover. You just need to learn how and apply what you learn.

OCD Mechanics

Understanding OCD

The one good thing about OCD, if you can call it that, is that it is very logical. There are simple reasons why you feel the way you feel, why you get the thoughts that you get and what makes these thoughts stay. In this chapter we will discuss this in-depth. I include this chapter in almost all of my books, because I want every person who reads my books to understand the mechanics of OCD. It is essential part of getting over OCD and it is nearly impossible to get over OCD without this information.

Why This Thought?

Almost every one of my clients has asked me that at some point. I asked myself when I had OCD, why am I having these specific thoughts? The reason is simple. Throughout the day you get many thoughts. Some are logical and some are not. Most of the time you are able to sort important thoughts from the unimportant. Your mind has no way to judge the thought fully and is looking to you, real you to judge it. It is basically throwing you a random thought and then it watches your reaction. If there is no strong reaction, the thought goes away never to come back. If the reaction is very strong the mind flags it as important. Then it repeats this important thought to you. If you continuously react to a thought, your mind will continue to send you more of this type of thought, no matter what the thought is. This mechanism is why you have this thought and ultimately why you have OCD. Sexual OCD thoughts are not different. It is just a thought being thrown at you that scares you. It is random and holds no deep meaning.

Think of your current OCD situation. How did it first start? You got a random thought and started to panic. You thought about it over and over again getting increasingly anxious as you thought of all the possibilities. The key part here is that you got a random thought but you chose to react with anxiety. I know that this was all on the subconscious level and you did not feel that you had a choice. I have gone through all this myself when I had OCD. Think of a different type of OCD obsession. Think about how the person reacts with extreme anxiety to an OCD trigger that you would never react to. You would not react to that obsession but that person does. This makes the reaction a choice. You chose to react because you were scared and you chose to not react to other types of OCD because they are not important to you and they don't scare you.

When you make the choice to react to a random thought with a lot of anxiety, your brain flags this thought as important and then sends it to you again. When it sends it again, you again react with a lot of fear. It takes note this second reaction and flags it as definitely important. Not only important, it flags it as dangerous since you are reacting with fear. Keep in mind that your brain does not understand that you have OCD, it thinks that the choice to react with anxiety to this type of thought comes from a real danger. So it will send you more variations of this same thought.

In short, the reason why you get this thought is because you are choosing to react to it with fear. OCD always attaches to what is the most important because if this was not important to you, you would not care enough to react with fear. It doesn't matter what type of OCD it is. Having Sexual OCD is not better or worse than any other type of OCD. It is all OCD, the topics do not matter.

Why does the brain do this?

The basic job of the brain is to protect the person from danger and to make them react when necessary. When you repeatedly pay attention to a certain type of thought and react to it with a lot of fear, your brain starts to "flag" this thought as danger. Remember that it cannot judge the situation the way you can so it is looking for what you will do and how will you react. In case of Sexual OCD, it sends you a sex-related thought and looks to you to see how you react. If you react with indifference, the thought goes away never to come back. If you react as if it is important, it will send you more of these thoughts.

So the question is really not why you are having this type thought but why do you choose to react to this type of thought? Anyone can get it but not every one will react to it with fear. The reason why you react with fear to this thought is that this thought attacks what is the most precious to you. This is different for everyone and so there are different types of OCD. Some people worry about health and may develop contamination OCD, family oriented people may worry about something happening to their family, money oriented people will worry about their finances.

I case of Sexual OCD, the reason why you are having these thoughts is because you are a nice person with high morals and principles. This is very important to you. To you, a Sexual OCD thought is the worst possible thought you could have, so you react to it, which starts the cycle of OCD.

These thoughts mean nothing. They say nothing about you as a person. The only reason you are having them, is because it attacks what is the most precious to you. You can reprogram your mind to send you only the thoughts that you want. To do this you need to continuously show your mind that the OCD thoughts you receive are not important to you. Your mind is set up to only send you important thoughts, so as soon as you signal to your mind that these thoughts are not important, it will start to reprogram itself. It is important to continuously use this technique, so your brain sees the same pattern again and again. The more stability your brain sees in your actions, the faster you will recover. Your brain equates calm stability to safety. If you react without any fear to all the OCD thoughts, your brain will understand that there is no danger attached to this type of thought/situation and will stop sending these thoughts to you.

Reassurance, Compulsions And Avoidance

There are three main types of behaviors that most people with OCD engage in. These behaviors are reassurance, avoidance and compulsions. All three are in reality forms of reassurance. Reassurance is basically making sure you are safe. In terms of Sexual OCD, this means seeking reassurance that you have not done or thought anything wrong. Avoidance is reassurance you do before the event to reassure yourself that the thought is not true. Compulsions reassure you that you that everything is OK. All these behaviors are forms of reassurance that further OCD.

What is reassurance?

Reassurance is any action done specifically to neutralize OCD thought and make sure you are not in danger. This action can be physical, such as turning light switch on and off or mental such as rumination and trying to solve thoughts. It's important to note that reassurance is normal human behavior and is not bad in general. It only becomes a problem when the act of reassurance is done for the sole purpose of reducing OCD.

In Sexual OCD, reassurance often involves thinking back to the situation to remember if anything sexual has happened. If your fears are about the future, you may engage in analyzing yourself and your actions in order to make sure you will not do anything. If your fears are about the past and you also have False Memory OCD, you most likely spend a lot of time examining your actions to make sure you have not done anything sexual. There are many examples of reassurance but these are very common ones that I see every day when talking to clients.

Harm In Reassurance

Remember that your mind is a machine. The problem with reassurance is that the part of the mind that is responsible for sending you more thoughts does not have the ability to understand whether the thoughts are valid or not, or even the content of them. The only way it can judge the thoughts is by your reaction to them. It looks for your reaction to see if something is important or not. So the machine is basically looking to you to see if the thought is important.

When you seek reassurance you are telling your brain that this thought is important, because a person does not seek reassurance from meaningless thoughts. So, if you react as if it is important, it will send you more thoughts in order to bring something "important" to your attention. If you react as if it is not important, it will stop sending you these types thoughts. That is the simple mechanism that becomes a problem when overcoming OCD.

Reassurance From Self

Self-reassurance is the most common type of reassurance. It is present in everyone who has OCD. This one is always the toughest one to get rid of. It is always present with Sexual OCD. You can stop yourself from physically going and asking someone, but it's hard to refuse thinking about something.

The person can spend hours analyzing the thoughts to try to figure out if the thought or situation is real or not. Every time you engage in analyzing you are sending a signal to your mind that this thought is important.

This type of reassurance is especially important to overcome. That is because when you seek reassurance from another person, this is a single event and therefore a single signal being sent to your mind. So, even if you went and asked for reassurance from someone, that's just +1. With self-reassurance, you are basically constantly asking yourself if the thought is true, so it's +1000's of signals. You have to focus on eliminating this type of reassurance. Do mental checks. Where are your thoughts now? Are you analyzing? Are you looking into the details? If you are, this is a step back and you need to get back to recovery.

Example of Sexual OCD reassurance from self

"What if I something sexual in this particular situation?" Logically I know I didn't but I feel, what if I did? I better think about it to try and figure out if the thought is true. The person will spend long periods of time going over the situation to try and solve it. This means the person is trying to get reassurance from within the self by trying to remember the situation. This is connected to False Memory OCD.

Example of Sexual OCD reassurance from others

"What if I something sexual in this particular situation?" Logically I know I didn't but I feel, what if I did? I need to ask someone about his or her opinion. I already asked before, but I need to ask again just to make sure everything is OK. If you are seeking reassurance from others you also may find it more comfortable to not be alone so you have a witness who you can ask later. If this is the case, try as much as possible to refuse these OCD patterns. Remember that even if you get over this OCD thought you will get another one just like this because your mind is finding this situation important and the root of this is reassurance.

Reassurance and Avoidance

Avoidance is reassurance that takes place before the situation even happens. By avoiding you are refusing to put yourself in the situation that may give you OCD. It is still reassurance and you are sending your brain a signal that this situation is dangerous, when it isn't. You are basically saying to your mind that this situation is dangerous for you and you have to avoid it. This confuses your mind and makes OCD worse in the long term because now every time you are in this similar situation in the future, your mind will send you anxiety so you protect yourself.

Example of Sexual OCD Avoidance

A common example of Sexual OCD is standing close to people, because the sufferer worries that he or she may touch them.

The more the person avoids the more the person feels the need to avoid other things as well. At first the person may only avoid being alone with another person, then after some time the worry may spread to not being able to be around people even in groups. It may get to a point where the person may be afraid to leave their house at all.

Reassurance and Compulsions

A compulsion is done to ensure that the feared situation did not happen in the past, to undo it or prevent it from happening in the future. Compulsion can be mental, physical or both. In each case the person does the compulsion to reassure himself or herself that the feared situation is not a threat. At its core, any compulsion is a way to seek reassurance.

The brain sends a thought in order to see if the person will react with fear. Doing any type of reassurance sends a fear response to your brain, because you are protecting yourself from "danger". Your brain sees that you are doing things you would not normally do because you are scared. It doesn't understand OCD and mental disorders; it is programed to associate fear response with actual danger, which is not true if the person has OCD.

If your brain receives the fear response from you, it will send you more of these thoughts in order to try to protect you from this "danger". You start to worry about this thought and the "what if" future outcomes if the thought is true. The more you worry, the more your mind views this as an important thought and tries to send you even more similar thoughts. It does this because it received a signal of danger from you and is trying to get you to react to this signal.

The more you react with fear, the more of this thought it will send. It may also try to send you similar thoughts within the same "theme" because if you reacted with fear to this thought, maybe other similar thoughts are important and dangerous as well.

Remember that your brain does not understand that the thoughts are not important. It only understands your reaction of fear.

Now lets take a look at how a person who doesn't have OCD handles a Sexual OCD thought. The person without OCD gets a thought, for example let's say that the thought is about touching someone as he or she walks by them. A person who doesn't have OCD logically knows that there is no evidence that something is wrong, so he or she chooses to disregard it. The person does not allow the worry to overwhelm them and does not do any reassurance and avoidance. He or she does not ask what if, but simply sees the thought as silly and not important. The brain "sees" that and moves on.

Now compare that with a person who has OCD and how they react. It's easy to see why the brain gets confused.

I have helped a lot of people overcome OCD and I can tell you that there is no way you can overcome OCD until you stop seeking reassurance from these thoughts, both from yourself and from other sources.

Please understand that just because a thought feels real and comes with a lot of strong emotions such as guilt, shame and anxiety, it does not mean that it is true. OCD "sticks" to the person by these feelings. It has no logic but always feels as if it's real. If it didn't feel real you would not have OCD, you simply would not believe it.

The reason why it feels real and you get these emotions is that your brain thinks that the thought is real because you are acting and seeking reassurance as if it's real. So it sends you emotions that it would send if the thought was real. You get these emotions, get even more scared and send your brain even stronger signal of danger. Your brain gets this stronger signal of danger and creates even stronger negative emotions.

The good news is that through reassurance you have complete control of your OCD. If you keep doing reassurance you keep OCD going. If you stop reassurance you stop OCD.

If you are feeling bad today, you probably were seeking reassurance a short while ago, so the brain is sending you more thoughts.

To recover from OCD you need to stop all reassurance. When you do that, your mind will eventually stop viewing this type of situation as a problem and will stop sending you these thoughts. It won't happen overnight because your mind is used to this way of thinking, but it will happen. Your job is to keep reinforcing day after day, moment after moment that this situation is not important. Your mind will eventually get it and move on. When the next thought comes into your mind, say:

This is my usual OCD theme. I choose to not think about this. I choose to view this as OCD. If one day it turns out not to be

OCD, I will deal with it then, but right now I choose to view it as OCD. I refuse to think about this any further and I will not get into the details. I am choosing to move on.

After saying this, refocus your mind on real life situations. Keep busy and keep refocusing all day.

Recovery Process for Sexual OCD

Now let's talk about how long it will take you to recover. You may have already read this in my other books, but I find that this is very important to include in all my books because this is the question I get asked again and again. Sexual OCD recovery is not different from any other type of OCD, therefore the recovery process is the same as well. The recovery time with OCD is completely dependent on how well you can refuse to pay attention to the thoughts. Paying attention means seeking reassurance that everything is OK. I know that up until now you were not very successful at this, but you also didn't fully understand how OCD works and what makes the thoughts go away. Now that you know how it works, you should have much easier time disregarding the thoughts.

How Long Will It Take To Recover

On average people take about six months to recover using my method. The recovery time fully depends on how well you learn to control your thoughts and the amount of effort you put into recovery. Reassurance is your number one problem. If you tackle it every moment of every day you will see results fast. If you do very little, you will take a very long time to recover. It's all completely up to you. I have helped people who recovered from severe OCD in just a few months. I also tried to help people recover who simply refused to give up reassurance and those people did not recover while talking to me. You have to be ready for hard work.

If you put maximum effort into recovery you should start to see progress almost right away.

Progress in OCD means that you have less anxiety throughout the day. Don't judge the progress day to day, instead judge week to week. Day to day is not accurate because you may just be having a bad day and forgot how you should treat an OCD thought. It could be due to stress or unexpected situations. If you failed for one day it's not a problem. You will bounce back the next day. It is a problem in recovery if you have been reacting to the thought the wrong way for a week or longer.

How Can You Tell That You Are Recovering

When you start to follow the advice given, you will see that your thoughts will start to switch very quickly. They may still relate to Sexual OCD or may even switch themes entirely. Although it may feel overwhelming, this is a good sign and it means that your brain is not getting fully attached to a single thought. It goes from thought to thought because you are refusing to take the thoughts seriously and the thoughts can't attach to you for very long.

The brain will send you a thought - you refuse to believe it. Then it sends you another one; you refuse to believe that one as well. If you do everything right they will switch in this manner. The reason why the brain will do this is because it is used to you focusing on a single thought and having a lot of anxiety. If you refuse the anxiety, it thinks you are doing something unsafe and will try to send you more similar thoughts to get you to react.

After awhile, it will "understand" that everything OK and will stop sending you OCD thoughts. This is the process of recovery. The only difference between a person who has OCD and a person who does not, is how they react to the thoughts. The more you choose to react like someone who doesn't have OCD, the faster you will recover. Remember, if it has to do with harm, it is OCD and you are moving on.

Does Everyone Recover?

No, unfortunately not everyone recovers. To recover you need to start reducing your reassurance behaviors, in all of their forms. If you reduce them quickly you will recover quickly. If you reduce them slowly, you will recover slowly. One is not better than the other and both will get you to the same finish line. If however you do not reduce your behaviors, or if you reduce some but keep others, you will not recover. This is the truth, you need to be brave and refuse to buy into the OCD fears. The chart below illustrates the process of recovery.

SPEED OF OCD RECOVERY PROCESS

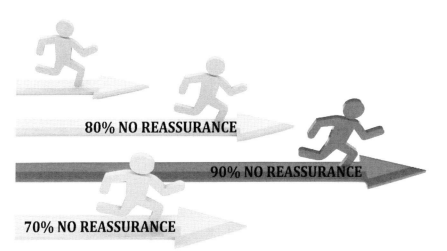

THE LESS REASSURANCE YOU SEEK, THE FASTER YOU WILL RECOVER

Life After Recovery From OCD

What happens after recovery?

After recovery you will go back to your normal character. OCD does not change who you are no matter what kind of thoughts you have. You will be generally the same person you were before you developed OCD, just a little more knowledgeable about OCD and more compassionate and sensitive to other people because of all you went through. You will no longer have Sexual OCD thoughts plaguing you. You simply will not worry about this topic. Other than that, you will be exactly the same as before you developed OCD.

Does it go away suddenly?

It is a gradual change. Most people cannot identify the exact day or week that their OCD goes away. For me, I had severe OCD attacks right when I would wake up or if I was spending a lot of time by myself. As I started to recover, I noticed that more and more days I would wake up free of OCD worries. Also I noticed more and more that some days I did not get OCD thoughts. As I continued to recover these days would multiply and the OCD days diminished and eventually got to a point where I rarely got an OCD thought. From that point they went away completely.

Will I still have worries?

Yes, you will still have worries, you will not experience worry free life, at least not the majority of us. The worries will be there but they will not be OCD based, they will be real life situations and the level of worry will not be nearly as intense. Basically, you will feel the same as everyone else.

Can OCD come back?

Yes, OCD can come back. Especially if you experience any type of extreme stress later in life, your brain might feel threatened and send you an OCD thought, either based on the past theme or an entirely new theme. The good thing is that after you do all the recovery work needed to overcome OCD, you will be able to easily tell that the thought is OCD and dismiss it. Your biggest advantage in the war against OCD is knowing the enemy. Once you know how it functions and what makes it go away, you will never fall for it again. So it may try to come back but it doesn't mean you will let it, especially after going through the process of recovery.

If you have a fear and it is lasting longer than it would for anyone you know, if they were put in the same situation, this means it is OCD. Any thought that is giving you unnecessary fear should be dismissed as quickly as possible.

OCD Emergency Plan

Step 1 – Why Am I Feeling Worse?

List all the reassurances that you have been seeking for this specific situation in the very resent past. Make sure to include all the reassurance behaviors including self-reassurance and avoidance.

Step 2 – My Plan For The Day

Write as many things as you want, the more the better. The busier you are, the less energy you will have to worry about the thoughts.

Step 3 – Checkmark when done and rate your level of anxiety.

As you work on the things you plan, put a checkmark next to every project you finished. Note your level of anxiety.

-------------------------------------/ Anxiety Level_____

-------------------------------------/ Anxiety Level_____

-------------------------------------/ Anxiety Level_____

-------------------------------------/ Anxiety Level_____

-------------------------------------/ Anxiety Level_____

-------------------------------------/ Anxiety Level_____

-------------------------------------/ Anxiety Level_____

-------------------------------------/ Anxiety Level_____

Why Sexual OCD

Sexual OCD may seem more severe than other types of OCD's simply because of topic. In fact, it is exactly the same in terms of how your brain sees these thoughts. The brain sees that you react strongly to these types of thoughts (signals), so it sends you more of them. It has no idea what these signals really mean and the deeper understanding of how and why. It is a simple mechanism. If you react with fear to a contamination situation, you can develop Contamination OCD. If you react with fear to sexual thoughts, you will get more of them and develop Sexual OCD. There is no "deep reason" why the brain is sending it, it is simply repeating the pattern of sending you the same type of thought, only slightly different.

Why This Specific Thought

The reason you have this specific thought has to do with your morals. People who have high morals or generally view these thoughts as extremely unacceptable are prone to developing this type of OCD. You are the complete opposite of these thoughts, that's why having these thoughts scares you. When you react with fear you send that signal of fear to your brain and start the pattern of OCD. In this case, Sexual OCD.

Can It Switch?

It can absolutely switch to a different type of OCD. The reason why you are stuck on Sexual OCD is because you are reacting to these types of thoughts and not others. When you get a strange thought on a different topic you simply brush it off. It doesn't stick to you. When you get a sexual thought, you take it seriously and with a lot of fear, so it sticks. As soon as you change which thoughts you are choosing to pay attention to, your brain implements these signals. Of course, it is not immediate recovery, but the brain does begin to let go of the idea that specifically Sexual OCD thoughts are dangerous or even important. As it continues to let go, you feel less anxiety until it fully goes away.

Feelings with Sexual OCD

I find that generally the reason why the person is afraid to disregard the thoughts, is the feelings that come along with the thought. I am listing most common feelings in this chapter so you can recognize them when they come to you and refuse any reaction to them. If you understand why you feel a certain way and how to stop it, it greatly reduces the fear around these thoughts.

Physical Sensations

Why You Feel This Way

Because we are talking about Sexual OCD, unwanted arousal is very common. This often scares people. You have to remember that the machine that is your brain thinks the thought is important. Since that machine also controls the rest of your body, it can give you physical sensations.

How To Stop It

View these physical feelings as nothing more than the brain giving you an error. It means nothing, just like the emotional feelings that you get with OCD. The less you take them seriously, the less they will appear.

Vivid Images

Why You Feel This Way

If you have False Memory OCD thoughts, you may feel stuck because of the vivid images that you get. You may worry how you can have these vivid images if the thought is not true. Again, because the brain is stuck in the wrong programming, your imagination comes up with images that will support the story. This is very common.

How To Stop It

Try to remind yourself that you and other people with OCD have had vivid images with many OCD thoughts, yet none ever turned out to be real. The less attention you pay to the images, the less vivid they will seem.

Feeling Guilt And Shame

Why You Feel This Way

The reason why you feel shame and guilt is because you are taking these thoughts seriously. There is nothing to be ashamed of, if you look at these thoughts as OCD. The fears are not true, there is simply nothing here to feel guilty about.

How To Stop It

To stop feelings of guilt and shame, you have to go after that emotion and show your mind that it is not valid. Every time you feel shame, say: " I refuse to believe it, I am moving on."

Feeling Like You Need To Confess To Someone

Why You Feel This Way

This is a reassurance behavior that helps the person feel better for a very short time. The brain wants you to make sure you are safe and if there is a way to figure out if something is valid or not through another person, you will get the urge to seek reassurance.

How To Stop It

To stop this feeling you need to refuse the urge to confess. No matter how much you feel you need to tell or ask someone, do not do it. If you do the reassurance you may feel better for a second, but it will come back worse because you are following OCD and basically saying to your mind that this is important. You have to stay strong and refuse.

Feeling Like You Need To Figure Out The Truth

Why You Feel This Way

The brain is trying to figure out if you are really in danger. It will keep sending the thoughts to you over and over again. It is not trying to torture you, it simply learned that this situation is important and is now sending you similar thoughts based on that programming in order to protect you. You need to prove to it that you don't need protection from this.

How To Stop It

Refuse trying to figure it out. If your mind sends you the urge to figure out the thoughts a million times, you have to refuse a million times. Imagine a goalie protecting the net. No matter how many balls are thrown at the net you have to protect it. The more you refuse figuring the thoughts out, the less anxiety you will experience, because the brain will start to adjust to new programming in which you are telling it that the thought is not important.

Feeling Like A Bad Person

Why You Feel This Way

These thoughts are the worst thoughts you could possibly have, that's why they are giving you OCD. If they were not the worst thoughts for you, they would not trigger you. This shows that you are a good person. Bad people can have OCD, but they will not have it about the topic that they feel is not bad. To get OCD about something, it has to go against who you truly are, so there is a conflict. Bad people don't have this conflict. They don't care that they are bad and because of that will not have OCD about being bad. They can still get OCD, but it will be about something completely different.

How To Stop It

Keep reminding yourself that many people experience exactly the same thoughts and feelings and nothing ever happened. There is no reason to pay attention to these thoughts. As much as you can continue to shift your attention away from trying to figure out if you are a good or a bad person.

Say: "I choose to believe that I am a good person. I don't care what OCD says. I am a good person and I refuse to pay attention to these thoughts."

The less fear you show, the faster your brain will adjust.

Feeling Alone

Why You Feel This Way

The truth is, even people with one type of OCD have great difficulty understanding other types of OCD. We all have to deal with our specific situations and if you look at it this way, we all are alone. No one can understand you the way you understand yourself. Even people who don't have OCD feel alone, like nobody understands them.

How To Stop It

I suggest simply accepting it as part of our reality. If you refuse paying attention to it, this feeling will greatly reduce.

Feeling Like I Am Not Worth Anything

Why You Feel This Way

This is another common feeling for people with OCD. Again, it comes from the fact that you think that these thoughts make you a bad person. The brain has learned this pattern and keeps throwing these feeling to you.

How To Stop It

Do the opposite of what OCD wants you to do in terms of self worth. For example, if you want to buy something for yourself but you feel that you are not worth it, buy it. At first it will be very challenging, view it as an exercise and continue until it no longer has any effect on you. By doing this you are showing your mind that these thoughts are false, which is exactly what you need to show.

Reassurance With Sexual OCD

As you read in the first part of the book, reassurance is the reason why OCD is not going away and is getting worse. Now let's take a look at some of the most common reassurance behaviors.

It is very important for you to identify all of the reassurance behaviors so you eliminate them.

Reassurance From Others

Reassurance from others means that you are trying to prove that the situation is not true by asking others. I am listing some common examples of this type of reassurance below.

- Asking people directly if the fear is valid.

- Trying to "read" the person by their actions to determine if the fear is valid.

- Asking the person indirectly, without really asking them.

- Interpreting what they say to figure out if the fear is true.

Reassurance From Self

Reassurance from self, means that you are trying to get reassurance that the fear is not true by mentally trying to solve or figure out the situation. Almost like solving a mathematical problem. Below are some variations of this behavior.

- Going over the situation to see if there is anything wrong.

- If the situation is from the past, remembering what happened to see if there was anything wrong.

- Using the Internet to help yourself solve the problem.

- Going on OCD forums to make sure that this is OCD.

- Trying to figure out if you are capable of doing something bad.

- Comparing yourself to other people.

Please understand that you cannot recover from OCD while you continue to do these behaviors. Every moment of every day, continue to make the effort to stop them.

Avoidance with Sexual OCD

As you now understand, the worst thing you can do is to seek reassurance. Part of reassurance is avoidance. There are a lot of avoidance behaviors that are common to Sexual OCD. I will talk about them in this chapter. I'm sure you will recognize a lot of them. I help a lot of people with OCD, and no matter where they are in the world, these behaviors are very common. Not everyone has every single behavior that I will mention, but most of them are the same for everyone with this type of OCD.

Please remember that all of these behaviors are making your OCD worse.

- Avoiding certain people

- Avoiding being alone with people

- Avoiding talking about sexual topics

- Avoiding movies or show that can trigger OCD

- Avoiding sitting close to people

- Avoiding hugging or touching other people

- Avoiding certain places that can trigger your OCD

- Avoiding using certain words because they might be misinterpreted to be something sexual

All these behaviors may seem like they are protecting you from getting an OCD thought, but they are actually sending a signal to your brain that you are scared of these topics. This will make OCD worse in the long run and your brain will work even harder to give you another OCD thought.

Your brain has no way to stop on it's own, once it has been programmed. The only way to stop it, is to give it new programming.

Refocusing Attention

Your brain cannot simply stop thinking. It always needs something to do. If it doesn't have any tasks, it will find tasks on it's own. It uses old programming for that. Think of it as if it is a monkey that is trapped in a room. It has nothing to do, there are a lot of objects around that the monkey can throw around and make a big mess. Now what if you choose what the monkey can and cannot do? What if you train the monkey?

Why Some People Care And Some People Don't

Have you ever wondered why some people care so much about something and others barely even notice it? It is all about attention. The person chooses to give something a lot of attention and gets deeply emotionally involved. Another person refuses to give the thought attention and it goes away. To get over OCD you need to regain control where you choose to focus your attention.

Attention Drives Everything

Try to take notice where your attention is at all times. In case of Sexual OCD, when you spend time with a person or standing close to a person, is your attention on real life or is it on OCD fears? Attempt to shift it to real life every time it goes to these OCD thoughts. It will take time for your brain to learn this new pattern of behavior. Keep teaching it that these thoughts are not important by only putting your attention on important thoughts.

Using This Technique In Every Area Of Your Life

Think of how much attention and energy you give to things that are not important or bring negativity into your life. Try to use this technique of choosing where to put your attention in every area of your life. It is a skill and once you master it, your quality of life will greatly improve.

Subtypes of Sexual OCD

There are many subtypes of Sexual OCD. It is very important that you know about them so you understand that you are not alone. This is not happening only to you.

Millions of people experience these thoughts, and they are never true. This understanding will give you the power to see through the fears and refuse giving any attention to them.

Below are the most common combinations of Sexual OCD.

- False Memory OCD and Sexual OCD

- Harm OCD and Sexual OCD

- Contamination OCD and Sexual OCD

- Cheating OCD and Sexual OCD

- Homosexual OCD and Sexual OCD

- Philosophical OCD and Sexual OCD

- Religious OCD and Sexual OCD

- HIV OCD and Sexual OCD

- Health OCD and Sexual OCD

- Relationship OCD and Sexual OCD

As you can see, almost any type of OCD can intertwine with Sexual OCD.

I'm not going to give you specific examples of these OCD types because I don't want to trigger an OCD thought, but please understand that these thoughts are very common. They may seem scary but they are not unique. And no matter how scary they seem, they are not real.

My Partner Has Sexual OCD. What Should I Do?

If you are a partner of someone with Sexual OCD, do not panic. It is not different than any other type of OCD. Your partner is not a bad person, he or she just simply has OCD. Once OCD goes away, so will these thoughts.

If the thoughts are scary in their nature, it does not make your partner strange or a bad person. On the contrary, the fact he or she is so worries about these thoughts means that he or she is extremely against them. Most people don't care enough to worry so much. They simply disregard them. The fact that your partner finds them so wrong shows his or her high morals.

What Can You Do To Help?

As you read from the earlier chapters, OCD gets worse when the person does avoidance, reassurance and just generally gives a lot of attention to the thoughts. Since you spend a lot of time around your partner, you are the perfect person to help him or her. Below are the things you can do in each area of OCD.

Avoidance

If you see your partner trying to avoid something because of OCD, try to remind him or her that it is not a good idea in terms of recovery. Try to help your partner stop the avoiding behavior or at least reduce it.

Reassurance

If your partner asks you to reassure him or her, try to remind them that it is not a good idea. If you feel that you cannot stop them from asking for reassurance you can make a deal with them that you will only allow one reassurance per day, then reduce it to one per week and further until it is gone.

Analyzing, Thinking About OCD Topics

If you see that your partner is thinking about OCD, try to remind him that he or she is making it worse by engaging the thoughts. A gentle reminder can really help them in the moment to remember to stop actively reacting to the thought.

The most important thing is to remind them that they are hurting their progress by seeking reassurance.

Sexual OCD FAQ

Is Sexual OCD harder to get over than other types of OCD?

Absolutely not, even though it seems like it is more severe than other types of OCD to the person who is suffering with it, the level of anxiety is the same and therefore the recovery is the same. What makes a difference in terms of recovery is your willingness to disregard the thoughts no matter how real they feel and how much anxiety they send you.

Does this type of OCD say anything about me as a person?

If you have this type of OCD it means that you have high morals and you are a very good person. OCD generally attacks what is the worst possible thing for the person. Some people get Religious OCD, some get Harm OCD and some get Sexual OCD. Since you are a good person, the worst thing for you is this types of thoughts/fears. That's why OCD gets attached to it.

Should I be in a relationship if I have sexual OCD?

If you are already in a relationship, do not end your relationship because of your OCD. If you are thinking of getting into a relationship, I would suggest to wait until you are further into your recovery. The only reason I suggest to wait is because you may find it very hard to be in a relationship in the beginning or your recovery when your anxiety is extremely high. This period does not last long.

Should I tell my partner about my OCD?

I have a lot of experience helping people with Sexual OCD, and there is a pattern that I always see in relationships where one of the partners has OCD. The other partner does want to help, they know that their loved one is suffering. Even though he or she wants to help, if they are asked repeatedly for reassurance it gets to be too much very quickly. For this reason I would suggest to tell your partner that you have OCD, but not get into great detail. You may feel like you want to "confess" all your thoughts, but this is just OCD reassurance.

I have thoughts about people that are constantly around me. Should I avoid them?

The more you avoid them, the higher your anxiety will be the next time you are around them. Absolutely do not avoid. By facing these people you are sending a clear signal to your brain that there is no real danger. Use it as an exposure exercise. After you spend time with them, you may get what if thoughts. Keep refusing to react and these thoughts will go away. Remember that exposure does not instantly mean recovery. You have to expose yourself to the situation, and refuse OCD reaction, only when you refuse will your brain "see" that there is no dager and will stop sending you the thoughts.

I have feelings of arousal that come with my OCD thoughts, what does it mean?

There is a reason why this is happening. The reason is that overtime, as you reacted with a lot of fear to these thoughts, your brain learned to take them seriously. The brain controls the entire body, including your arousal, so it can trigger it even though you are feeling disturbed by these thoughts. This is common with this type of OCD and it does go away as the brain learns that the situation is not valid.

I am afraid to discuss this topic with my doctors or anyone else. What do you advise?

You have to be careful who you talk to about this. Not all doctors are knowledgeable about OCD. Specially because the topic is very sensitive, you have to be cautious. When you tell another person anything, they now have information to use in any way they want. If they don't understand OCD they may think that there is something else happening in this situation. Usually most people are very understanding about these thoughts and can easily tell that they are not valid, but I would still advice to be cautious.

Should I avoid sex while I am getting over this type of OCD?

You should not change your life in any way because of OCD. When you do something specifically because of OCD, you show your brain that OCD thoughts are important. This is the opposite of what you want to show. Based on this, if you are having sex then do not stop because of OCD. Also, if you are not having sex, do not do it specifically because of OCD. Generally OCD should not be a factor in your decision making process.

I have False Memory OCD that is connected to Sexual OCD, is this common?

Yes, many times the main worry would be what if something happened with another person. I encounter this type of OCD more than any other type. You may get vivid images that come with this type of OCD combination. You have to disregard them all and choose to move on.

My Sexual OCD thoughts are connected to Cheating OCD, is this common?

Yes, this is common and just like in the previous question, can be connected to False Memory OCD. Try to have it as a rule, that any anxiety provoking sexual thought is OCD, and refuse to look into the details.

Does alcohol make OCD worse?

Yes, it does make OCD worse because in addition to getting regular OCD thoughts, you may get a thought that what if I was too drunk to remember. This never actually happens to people who have this type of OCD, but the fear will be there.

Can Sexual OCD switch?

Yes, it can easily switch to another type of obsession. This usually happens when the person's situation changes. For example, if a person was in a relationship and had strong Sexual OCD thoughts connected to that relationship, and then suddenly the relationship ended, OCD theme might switch to another topic. The important part here is that the level of anxiety will remain the same, just the topic will change.

Can you have more than one type of OCD at the same time?

Usually people have a primary theme and a secondary theme. For example, most of the time the person has Sexual OCD worries but also has minor Checking OCD compulsions.

My thoughts have False Memory OCD theme, some of them come instantly after a situation and some are from a long time ago. Is this common?

I actually have a separate book on False Memory OCD. It can happen anytime, either right after the situation or long after. It's just another way thoughts get stuck in the mind, but they are still OCD thoughts.

I had this OCD for a long time, can I still recover if I have been suffering this long?

Yes, you can recover no matter how long you suffered with it. Sometimes I see people who have not had it for a long time and have a hard time overcoming OCD, other times I see people who have had it for years and are so sick of it that they fight it with everything they have and overcome it. It's not about time, it's about determination to refuse these thoughts no matter how real they seem.

TV triggers my OCD. Should I avoid watching shows that trigger OCD?

This is again the same question as before about sex, the more you avoid the scarier it will be because your brain will understand your avoidance to mean that there is something wrong. However, I would not suggest watching shows that specifically deal with this topic unless you are ready to do exposures. I have a separate book written on exposures, but basically you have to be ready to face these thoughts so you react correctly. An incorrect reaction of fear will send a signal to your brain that this is important which will be a step back in your recovery.

My Sexual OCD is about the most inappropriate topics, is this common?

OCD always attaches to the worst fear, if it didn't then you would not react with anxiety and you would not develop OCD.

Start Now

The best place to start switching your brain is to focus on what is bothering you the least and slowly work up to what is bothering you the most. As you get rid of the lower-level obsessions, the higher-level ones will begin to seem less scary.

In the area below, write all the behaviors that you have because of OCD in the order from least scary to most scary. For the first few weeks, focus on the ones that are giving you the least anxiety. Don't move up to the level until you are fully confident in that you are over the one you are currently working on. The timing for this will be different for everyone. If you are not sure, that means you are not ready to move up to the next level.

What Is An OCD Behavior?

OCD behavior is any behavior that is done specifically to reduce OCD anxiety. This behavior can be mental in nature such as remembering something, analyzing the situation or trying to solve it.

Reassurance can also be physical such as doing physical compulsions or asking someone if something happened. OCD behavior can also be avoidance, meaning you are choosing to avoid the situation because it will trigger your OCD.

Generally, if you doubt any behavior as OCD, it most likely is OCD. Try not to follow what OCD wants you to do and do what you would normally do instead. It will increase you anxiety temporarily, but it also will send a signal to your brain that this is normal and there is no need to be anxious. This changes how your brain views the situation and next time when you are put in this situation you will have less anxiety.

Please use the example below to correctly fill out the chart. The most important thing is that you list all of your OCD behaviors with correct level of anxiety.

Determining Your Level Of Anxiety

In the chart below you will see that you need to sort your compulsions based on your level of anxiety. This means what your level of anxiety would be if you did not do the compulsion. Sometimes, the same compulsion can have multiple levels of anxiety depending on the circumstances. In this case you want to list it multiple times.

Is This Compulsion Still Bothering You?

Obviously when you begin, all your compulsions are still valid. As you progress in your recovery, use this space to check mark all compulsions that you already overcame.

Example for someone with Sexual OCD:

10/10 Taking time to remember what if anything sexual happened with another person.

Level of Anxiety / Reassurance Behavior

1/10(least scary)_____

1/10_____

1/10_____

1/10_____

2/10_____

2/10_____

2/10_____

2/10_____

3/10_____

3/10_____

3/10_____

3/10_____

4/10_____

4/10_____

4/10_____

4/10_____

5/10_____

5/10_____

5/10 _____

5/10 _____

6/10 _____

6/10 _____

6/10 _____

6/10 _____

7/10 _____

7/10 _____

7/10 _____

7/10 _____

8/10 _____

8/10 _____

8/10 _____

8/10 _____

9/10 _____

9/10 _____

9/10 _____

9/10 _____

10/10 _____

10/10 _____

10/10 _____

10/10 (most scary)_____

Completing Monthly Results Sheet

When filling out your monthly results sheet, you should pay special attention to the level of anxiety and the number of thoughts. If the level of anxiety is going down and the number of thoughts is going up, this means that you are progressing, as you should be. Remember that the reason you are getting more thoughts is because your brain is seeing that you are changing how you view these thoughts and is trying to send you every possible thought within your theme to ensure that you are not overlooking anything. This hyper-activity will pass.

The most important thing is that no matter how many thoughts you are getting, they should not be "sticking" to you. If the thought comes but does not stick, you will have lower levels of anxiety. High anxiety only happens when you allow the thought to develop further by actively engaging it. You want to see how fast one thought replaces another, because that will give you perspective on how strongly they "attach" to you.

Why am I not progressing?

If you are following the suggestions in the book, but feel you are not progressing, there may be three reasons for that.

The first reason may be that you are overlooking some reassurance behaviors. This often happens with self-reassurance (analyzing) or avoidance patterns. I suggest re-examining your daily life to see if you are missing anything.

The second reason could be because you may feel that the fact that you still have anxiety means that there is no progress. Remember that the anxiety you are experiencing right now is there because of the attention you paid to the thought in the past. It doesn't matter, it is auto sent to you by your brain based on the past experience. If you are disregarding the thoughts right now, in the future you will have less anxiety. It takes time to undo all the old reassurance.

The third reason is the most obvious one, and it is basically that you are still actively seeking reassurance in large amounts. If this is the case, try to seek at least a little bit less reassurance today than yesterday. This includes self-reassurance. Pick yourself up now and as much as possible, keep trying to refuse seeking reassurance.

My OCD thought "theme" is switching, what is happening?

If you are doing well with disregarding the thoughts, your brain is starting to switch. In the first part of switching, your brain gets a signal that the topic is no longer important to you. In response, it will try to alter the thought a little to see if any aspects of it are important. It does this because it still views this type of situation as dangerous based on past reassurance and wants to make sure you are safe in all aspects of this worry. Sometimes it may switch themes completely, that usually happens if you outgrew the theme entirely or your circumstances have changed where the theme is no longer a part of your daily life. Because Sexual OCD also interlinks with other types of OCD, it may shift from one secondary theme to another.

You have to keep in mind that the switching of the themes means very little in terms of OCD recovery. If you are anxious because of a thought for long periods of time, you need to continue working on your recovery. If you keep working hard and disregarding the thoughts, you will recover.

Results Sheet

*10= highest anxiety possible, 0= no anxiety. Record your average level of anxiety for the particular day.

Thank you for reading this book. I hope you find it useful. For more information visit youhaveocd.com

Monthly Result Sheet

....	Level Of Anxiety ?/10*	Number Of Thoughts Throughout The Day	Average Time Spent Per Thought
Day 1			
Day 2			
Day 3			
Day 4			
Day 5			
Day 6			
Day 7			
Day 8			
Day 9			
Day 10			
Day 11			
Day 12			
Day 13			
Day 14			
Day 15			
Day 16			
Day 17			
Day 18			
Day 19			
Day 20			

Day 21			
Day 22			
Day 23			
Day 24			
Day 25			
Day 26			
Day 27			
Day 28			
Day 29			
Day 30			
Day 31			

*10= highest anxiety possible, 0= no anxiety. Record your average level of anxiety for the particular day.

Thank you for reading this book. I hope you find it useful. For more information visit youhaveocd.com

Made in United States
North Haven, CT
24 April 2023